KALEIDOSCOPE
Realizing The I Am In Each of Us

AuthorHouse™
1663 Liberty Drive
Bloomington, IN 47403
www.authorhouse.com
Phone: 833-262-8899

Because of the dynamic nature of the Internet, any web addresses or links contained in this book may have changed
since publication and may no longer be valid. The views expressed in this work are solely those of the author and do not
necessarily reflect the views of the publisher, and the publisher hereby disclaims any responsibility for them.

Any people depicted in stock imagery provided by Getty Images are models,
and such images are being used for illustrative purposes only.
Certain stock imagery © Getty Images.

This book is printed on acid-free paper.

ISBN: 979-8-8230-3043-4 (sc)
979-8-8230-3044-1 (e)

Library of Congress Control Number: 2024914849

Print information available on the last page.

Published by AuthorHouse 08/07/2024

authorHOUSE®

TABLE OF CONTENTS

KALEIDOSCOPE
Realizing The I Am In Each of Us

I AM AWAKE

"In this Divine awakening there seems to be an inner witness
who remembers that we came from a heavenly state."
Science of Mind, p. 465

When I was a child I would sleepwalk at night. I would wander aimlessly through the house. At times I've wandered through Life the same way. I had no direction, no focus, and no purpose. Today I am awake. I have awakened to the realization that I am a physical representation of the Divine. My words are empowered by the voice of God. Spirit's healing touch is channelled through my hands. Spirit's presence travels with me wherever I go.

Because I am awake, I see God's face right in front of me. My laughter awakens within me the joy of Spirit that courses through my veins. As I embrace another in a hug, I know I am holding God in my arms. I am the way Spirit is manifested here in the physical. I am the Truth that Spirit reveals in, as and through me. I am the Life, the clay that Spirit molds and forms in its own Divine image.

I am Awake . . .

I Am Bountiful

"We shall be cared for as the lilies of the field,
which live directly upon the Divine bounty."
Science of Mind, p. 432

With every breath I take, I'm reminded of the Source behind it and know I am bountiful. To keep count of the breaths I take in one day would exhaust me. When I dream a new dream, nurture a new idea, contemplate a creative thought, I'm showered in Spirit's creative bounty. I witness Spirit's bountiful presence all around me in a diversity of people, places and things.

Mother Nature taps into Spirit's bountiful energy to blanket us in beauty, with the wide variety trees, flowers, landscapes and wildlife, Spirit's endless supply is undeniable. We are blessed with every type of music, art and literature. The manner in which Spirit speaks to us is limitless. The advancements in healthcare prove Spirit's never ending bounty of healing. Scientists exhibit a bounty of discovery that closes the mouths of all pessimists and naysayers. Because of technology, we are living like characters in a sci-fi movie. As these words flow from me, I'm reminded of the raindrops falling from the sky, every blade of grass and every grain of sand. This world, this life is a grand buffet.

I Am Bountiful . . .

I Am Compassion

Compassion: "a sympathetic consciousness."
Merriam Webster's

When I was a child I would see the Jerry Lewis, M. D. Telethon on TV. I often wondered what drove this man to go nonstop for twenty-four hours in order to benefit these children. Spirit's compassion is alive and well within each one of us. It shows up as pink ribbons in support of Breast Cancer research. Spirit's compassionate voice sings out at benefit concerts like Farm Aid, in 1985. When this world experiences pain like Hurricane Katrina, Spirit's compassion kick starts the human heart into action. Every December people express Spirit's compassion in the form of Christmas Spirit. The Christ within gives to those who are less fortunate. The Christ compassion within us declares this truth, *I am here and I will never leave you.* There is no greater love than selfless service. Whatever you do for one, you do for all of us. We are One . . . Allow Spirit's compassion to embrace you, love you, forgive you, console you.

I Am Compassion . . .

I Am Desire

"The desire arises from the necessity of the
universe to become self-expressed."
Science of Mind, p. 195

Often times the word "desire" gets a bad rap. It does come up in discussions about sexual matters. True desire is about so much more. The Divine desire to create, to express, to love; it is this desire that birthed you and me. Divinity's desire made it possible for the first human being to live, breathe and walk on this earth. This desire is behind every great discovery. It was Infinite Desire that played music within Beethoven. This same creative desire guided the paint brush of Picasso. Spirit's desire planted the seed within Dr. Martin Luther King, Jr., known as "The Dream." This desire, this dream continues to remind us of the Truth of our being. We are One and the same. Because of this desire to live a better life, I put down the bottle for good. Let Spirit's desire lift you, carry you and inspire you. Be the channel for this desire to heal and transform. Divine desire within, continue to flow through me just as this ink flows through this pen.

I Am Desire . . .

I Am Eternal

"Form is temporary, but Mind is eternal."
Science of Mind, p. 101

I remember when I first heard the glorious news of eternity. Long after my physical body passes on, the true essence of my being will go on forever. The fear of death and damnation that had been draped across my shoulders dissipated like fog. Gone was the worry of having only one chance to get it right. This realization gave me a new sense of purpose. I truly am Spirit's representative here in the physical. Long after I end this adventure called Life, my thoughts, my words, my deeds will have an effect. Did I lift up, or tear down? Did I contribute to the hurting or the healing? Is the world better off since I have been here?

Spirit's Love, Peace and Joy is the eternal flame within us that can never be extinguished. Divine Spirit within me, your presences is my essence. May your life, which is my Life right here, right now leave this world forever changed. And so it is!

I Am Eternal . . .

I Am Flesh

"In my flesh shall I see God."
Science of Mind, p. 330

In my experience, the word "flesh" has always had a negative energy attached to it. "Sins of the flesh" is a phrase I heard often as a child. Being human deemed on guilty simply by association. I used to apologize for my thoughts and feelings. I thought it was wrong to have my wants, needs, desires. Ironically, when I faced my demons, I was introduced to my Creator. I have seen God's face in the form of friends, teachers and mentors. Spirit's hands and feet have walked with me on this path of self-discovery. During this process of accepting and embracing my humanity, any doubts of my divinity within have disappeared. Spirit within me, when your word unites with my flesh, I am reborn, renewed, rejuvenated. May the divinity and humanity within each of us confirm the existence of God here and now.

I Am Flesh . . .

I Am Gethsemane

"We have no record of Jesus asking God to do anything
except in the Garden of Gethsemane."

Science of Mind, p. 277

The greatest teacher who ever lived even had his moment of doubt. He asked the Creator about an easier, softer way to complete his mission. The Nazarene wondered if there was a less difficult path to reach his destination. I have had many Gethsemane moments over the years. I've spent a lot of time and energy bargaining with God. *Please, anything but that,* I've pleaded. I've gotten pretty creative with the deals I've attempted to make with Spirit. As the Great Example embraced His destiny, a man named Simon of Cyrene helped lessen the weight of his undertaking. Over the years there have been many people from Cyrene, who have lessened the weight of my journey. When my critics within and outside of me were screaming, I felt I was sinking into Gethsemane like quicksand. To every Simon and Simone I have met along the way, thank you. I will never forget those times when you picked me up, dusted me off and pointed me back in the right direction. You, my traveling companions, have been the greatest blessing of my life. My friends, as we walk this path together, it is not the Garden of Gethsemane that surrounds us, it is the Garden of Eden. Divine Spirit within me, you replace my fear and doubt with strength and courage. All I need do is simply ask.

I Am Gethsemane . . .

I Am Grace

"God shed its Grace on thee . . ."
America the Beautiful, Katharine Lee Bates

When I was growing up, I completed the sacraments. I was told this was necessary to receive Grace. Today, I know Grace doesn't have to be earned. For each of us, Grace is a part of our Spiritual DNA. God's Grace flows through us like electricity in a power line. This Grace is awakened within me when the warm sun touches my skin. I'm embraced by Grace in the hug of a trusted friend. Spirit's Grace consoles me in the understanding heart of another. I witness the shining light of Grace on the face of a new born. I experience the diversity of Grace in the vastness of nature. I'm showered with God's Grace in the form of forgiveness. I'm filled with the limitless supply of Grace known as prosperity. We are all vessels of Spirit's Grace here in the physical. Divine Spirit within, pour out your Grace to a world thirsting for Truth.

I Am Grace . . .

I Am Heaven and Hell

"It is done unto you as you believe."
Matthew 9:29

For years I did an excellent job of playing victim and martyr. It took a long time for me to figure out that my thinking and attitude determines my experience in every moment. What an empowering discovery! I can decide if my life is Utopia or never-ending misery. There is no dictator placing conditions upon me. Everything falls in line with my perspective. Change my perspective, and everything coincides with that. Contrary to popular belief, I don't buy the idea of Hell as a fiery pit, where I will lay forever. For me, Hell is feeling isolated from my Creator, myself and others. To feel as if I don't matter, that my life doesn't matter is a living hell. Whenever I ponder the thought that my life makes no difference, there is a burning within me that cannot be ignored. Heaven is as close as my breath. It is in my mind, my heart, my soul. I feel Heaven's breeze as Spirit whispers in my ear. As God's hand guides my pen across this page, I feel elevated into the clouds. Divine Spirit within me, remove the blinders from my Physical and Spiritual eyes, enable me to see the pearly gates in every person, every place and every moment. And so it is . . .

I Am Heaven and Hell . . .

I Am Impossible

"It is impossible to conceive of anything other than the
Word of God being that which sets power in motion."
Science of Mind, p. 69

"I'm only human." How many times have I uttered those words? It was always my favorite statement when missing the mark. Some choose to believe there is nothing to celebrate in being human. Divinity laughs in the face of this pessimism. The unforgiveable is forgiven. The perceived unlovable is offered love and compassion. Every time the world screams, "No you can't!," the Spirit within says, "Oh, yes I can." How is it possible for a person to take on an overwhelming challenge, when the easier, softer way smells, sounds and tastes so much sweeter? The Nazarene predicted, "These things you will do, and greater." *John 14:12* I am reminded of the declaration, "Behold! I make all things new." *Revelations 21:5* Yes, my friends; God has our back. Spirit within me, as our hands join in this Divine partnership, I leap from this ledge of infinite possibilities.

I Am Impossible . . .

I Am the Journey

"Life is a journey, not a destination."

Ralph Waldo Emerson

My parents got tired of hearing, "Are we there, yet?", as we drove to our vacation destination. As an adult, I can be preoccupied with the destination. My thinking can get littered with statements like, "I'll be happy when . . ." Or, "I'll be successful when . . ." I can wear myself out with glass-half-empty thinking. I realize now if Spirit had rushed me through the express lane of Life, like I wanted, I would have missed so much. If I would have been granted the detour, I would have cheated myself. The challenging parts of life are where I've met the most amazing people, visited the most incredible places and had the most memorable experiences. This, for me, sums up the mystery of Life. I'm glad God is driving the tour bus. Spirit within me, thank you for your balance that tempers my urge to see the end of this path. I'm having too much fun!

I Am the Journey . . .

I Am the Kingdom

"We are to seek the Kingdom first."
Science of Mind, p. 432

Growing up in traditional church, I heard many sermons about the Kingdom. I left church many Sundays saying, "I want to go there some day." My childhood image of the Kingdom was clouds, angels and beautiful music. As an adult, I wasted many years trying to earn my ticket to that mythical place in the sky. When the teacher from Nazareth told his original twelve students, "The Kingdom is at hand," *Matthew 3:2,* he was not pointing to a location on a map. What if the road to the Promised Land runs through skid row? One man's kingdom may be a room full of people sharing stories of experience, strength and hope. Any teacher knows her kingdom is at hand when she sees the faces of her students light up after another lesson learned. Every musician experiences the Kingdom with another song composed and played. Artists show us what the Kingdom looks like through his or her eyes. What does the Kingdom look like for you? I sit here with a glass of iced tea, listening to some of my favorite music. I take this pen in hand and say to my only constant, "You speak, and I will write." No King or Queen has ever been blessed with a greater throne than me.

I Am the Kingdom . . .

I Am Limitless

"We are dealing with that which is limitless."
Science of Mind, p. 86

When I watched *Star Trek* as a child, I was fascinated with the handheld communicators, space ships and all the high-tech gadgets. Now we have cell phones and the space shuttle. The computers we have today make the one in *Star Trek* seem obsolete. The teacher from Nazareth said, "The blind will see, and the lame will walk." *Matthew 11:15* Now we have Lasik surgery, and prosthetic legs. In the 1930s, one man decided alcohol would no longer run his life. Today, the support system he created continues to teach men and women how to live life sober. In the 1960s, one man had one dream, and the Civil Rights movement began. Today, boys and girls of every creed, every color walk hand in hand. The man we know as the Dalai Lama was exiled from his homeland. He chooses to live his life reminding us that love and forgiveness is always the solution. At one time, my only desire was to party and have fun. Now my only desire is to carry the message of love and forgiveness simply for the sake of passing it on. Who am I to doubt God? Show the world your limitless potential. Come on; I dare ya! Spirit is the carpenter; we are its hammer and nails. Divine architect within, make me an example of your limitless potential.

I Am Limitless . . .

I Am Manna

"His hunger can only be satisfied
with Spiritual food, as manna from Heaven."
Science of Mind, p. 428

I'm reminded of that line from the Lord's Prayer; "Give us this day our daily bread." *Matthew 6:11* When I first learned this prayer, I thought we were all asking God to keep our bellies full. I eventually figured out that the emptiness I felt inside had nothing to do with the dinner table. I tried every remedy this world has to offer, but to no avail. I sought out fulfilment through work. Maybe I would feel more comfortable in my own skin if I had some important title? Life would be worth living once I acquired all the possessions I desire, right? If I find the right love relationship, I will feel whole and complete. It was unfair of me to expect another human being to be that which Spirit is meant to be. My peers had taught me I had been trying to fill a God-size hole within me with everything but that. So, what is my daily bread—my manna from Heaven? How am I being fed each day? My life feels empty without a purpose. I need to feel like I am part of the solution. Without my connection to my Creator, I feel lost. Through my relationships with trusted friends and peers, I experience Spirit's love, guidance and support. What is your source of manna? How are you being fed each day? Divine Spirit within me, thank you for my manna from Heaven, which is my purpose, my relationships, my life.

I Am Manna . . .

I Am Now

"Now is the closest approximation of eternity that this world offers."
A Course in Miracles, p. 247

He said this, and she said that. What if this happens? Then, I know that will happen, as well. It's no wonder life felt like something to be endured. One moment I was a prisoner to the regrets and resentments of the past. The next moment, I was paralyzed with fear, expecting the absolute worst in my future. I wasn't really living. I was a walking zombie, begging someone or something to put me out of my misery. For me, this insanity was all about control, and control is always about me wanting to feel safe. It did not matter if the outcome was misery; I felt safe having control of the outcome. I am tired of living life as a zombie. I want to live with the joyful exuberance that can only be experienced in the Now. Watch children; they will help you remember how to live in the now. Right now, I am safe. Right now, I am at peace. Right now, I feel Spirit's joy within me. Right now, I forgive everyone, including myself, for any perceived transgressions. Right now, I choose love. Right now is all I have. Right now, I have everything. Right now, Spirit walks this earth in, as and through me.

I Am Now . . .

I Am Opportunity

"We exist in limitless opportunities,
which are forever seeking expression through us."
Science of Mind, p. 291

I wanted life to come with a 100 percent guarantee. I wanted to try things, with no risk of failure. Well, I never got that guarantee; so, I wouldn't take risks. This is not fully living. This is being a prisoner to my own fears. Can you imagine where our society, our world would be if no one ever took a risk? We would still be living in caves. My thinking on this needed a major overhaul. No more black and white, right or wrong, good or bad, succeed or fail. Just as water is always wet, I am One with Spirit. This never changes, no matter what. This realization changed my life. Suddenly, each new day equalled a new opportunity; an opportunity to learn and grow as a person, an opportunity to make a new discovery, an opportunity to make a difference, an opportunity to be the change, be the solution, to simply be. Imagine walking into a casino and being granted an unlimited line of credit. Everything you win is yours to keep. Any losses are wiped clean, and you start off fresh. Worst-case scenario; you go out with what you came in with. Best-case scenario; at the end of your visit, you walk away with countless treasures. This can be my life, if I choose. Divine Spirit within me, you are my casino chip of opportunities. I know you have my back, always. I'm ready to take flight.

I Am Opportunity . . .

"A strong feeling of enthusiasm or excitement for
something or about doing something."
Merriam Webster on Line

Passion: Divine passion, physical passion. The latter has introduced me to all sorts of interesting adventures. True passion is sourced by the divinity within each of us. This level of passion goes beyond human understanding. It was this level of passion the teacher from Nazareth took beyond the grave. People like Gandhi, Mother Theresa and Dr. King experienced this same level of passion. Today, the Dalai Lama displays this passion through his words, his mission and his presence. It is Divine passion that pushes this pen across this paper. These are not my words; these are God's words. I am only a channel. I see Spirit's passion for beauty in nature. I hear Spirit's passion in music. I sense Spirit's passion for creativity in art. I acknowledge Spirit's passion for the miraculous in the face of every new born. Spirit's passion expresses through us like a kaleidoscope. It is the same light, yet it looks different on each of us; always unique, always beautiful, always Spirit. What is your passion? Just like splashing paints onto a canvass, put your passion on display for the world to see.

I Am Passion . . .

I Am Quiet

"From the eternal stillness, quietness and confidence are mine."
Science of Mind, p. 361

The squeaky wheel gets the grease. I have been taught to be bold, aggressive, the first in line. I believed that was the only way to get ahead in life. "You better get yours before it's gone." "Don't be passive, unless you want to be trampled underfoot." "Be on guard, ready to defend yourself." This mind set was grounded in fear, fear I would lose something I believed I possessed, fear I would not obtain what I thought I needed. It takes real courage not to raise my fist. It takes Spirit's wisdom to hold my tongue. If the Nazarene had spoken up and fought his oppressors, would his mission have had the same impact on the world? Gandhi declared himself a soldier of peace. Look at what he accomplished without raising a hand or raising his voice. Dr. King encouraged nonviolent protest. Some believe taking up the sword is the only way to be heard. If I were unable to speak, what would my life say on my behalf? With pen and paper in hand, Spirit whispers in my ear, and I write. This quiet solitude is my sanctuary, that Divine Source that I cannot live without. When I am quiet, I feel God's Love. When I am quiet, I hear God's wisdom. When I am quiet, I witness God's miraculous power.

I Am Quiet . . .

I Am Realization

"A constant realization of the presence of Spirit will provide the sense of Divine companionship that no other attitude could produce."
Science of Mind, p. 276

Every human being knows what it is to live and learn. My life has been a series of ongoing realizations. Some prefer the term "Spiritual awakening." Some of these realizations have changed my life, changed me as a person, and will stay with me after my transition. One such awakening was the day I realized not only that God can restore my peace, happiness and joy, but that God wants this for me. A weight lifted from my shoulders when I realized Spirit is not a tyrant, keeping score and dishing out punishment. All Spirit wants is to love me and be loved in return. Out of this awakening, I realized this exchange of giving and receiving love happens in, as and through my brothers and sisters. Each one of us is the face, hands and feet of God. In the form of flesh and blood, skin and bone, Spirit walks beside me in every moment. Through a trusted friend, my Creator listens to my concerns and offers words of wisdom. And, above all else, I realized the importance of caring for myself. I cannot be a channel of God's love and despise myself at the same time. Love, nurture and protect yourself as you would your own child. Sometimes words of hate and ridicule will enter your mind from your inner critic and critics around you. When this happens, cleanse the mind just as you would cleanse your body after ingesting poison. The realization of the divinity within me is the antidote for the poison of self-hatred. I know there is One Source, One Power, One Love. I know this presence surrounds me and permeates every part of me. I know Spirit's mind is one with my mind. I know because of this unity, Spirit speaks, acts and loves through me. Therefore, I realize we are all sons and daughters of God. Every human being is a member of that Royal Family called Divinity.

I Am Realization . . .

I AM SACRED

"Highly valued and important, deserving great respect."
Merriam Webster On Line

I remember the first time I held my new born niece and/or nephew. I was very aware of the sacredness of human life. I could clearly see the divinity within that little person. How exactly does one lose sight of the sacred within each person? A friend of mine, who is a mom, answered this question with one word; teenagers. Seriously, though, society does a great job of brainwashing all of us. Women and adolescent girls are told if they don't look like the Victoria's Secret ad, they are somehow less than. This is nonsense. I have witnessed many versions of beauty over the years. God does not make mistakes. As men, they hear, "Wear a Rolex; drive this type of car; wear these types of clothes." And, "I'd better have plenty of money, power and position." If not, there must be something missing from my resume. I believe success is part of a happy, healthy life. It is when my self-worth is contingent upon material things that it becomes unhealthy for me. Our Creator is sacred, therefore, we are sacred. Each of us is a unique copy of the Divine. Look past the distraction of our appearances and recognize the God qualities within every person. If Spirit were electricity, we would be its lightbulb. We are here to shine the Divine in the here and now. ". . . if God *was* one of us?" God is within each and every one of us. Look into the eyes of that other person and see the same eyes that stared at you from the crib. Divine Spirit within, I am here to speak your sacred word. I am here to pass on your sacred Love. I am here to reveal your sacred presence on this earth. For, thine is the Kingdom, the power and the glory.

I Am Sacred . . .

I Am Teacher . . .

"His whole teaching was that what he did, others could do."
Science of Mind, pp. 361-362

Ernest Holmes said the teacher from Nazareth was not the great exception; he was the great example. What if the Nazarene had said, "I'm just a carpenter's son. What can I offer?" I was taught, growing up, I wasn't worthy to unfasten his sandals. I was to wait for the man from Nazareth to come back and rescue me. This type of thinking does not serve our Creator or our world. Stop waiting for the next Jesus, Buddha, Mother Theresa, Gandhi or Dr. King. Spirit birthed you and I to be the change, be the difference, be the solution right here, right now.

The teacher from Nazareth did not want his students to be puppets or robots. He simply said, "Spread the good news." *Mark 16:15* It is the same beautiful message no matter what unique, diverse way you deliver it. Spirit's natural state is Love. We are the living, breathing manifestation of that same Love. Each of us has a choice, an opportunity. I can teach someone how to fish and enable that person to be fed for a lifetime.

I Am Teacher

I AM UNBELIEVABLE

"It is all so simple that it seems unbelievable."
Science of Mind, p. 417

I remember when the facilitator of my Science of Mind study group told me I am God in physical form. That statement terrified me. I thought, *when the cups of Kool aide are passed out, I'm outta here!* To say the least, it took a while to wrap my mind around this principle. The teacher from Nazareth said, "It is done unto you as you believe." *Matthew 9:29* The teacher was no magician. His belief was as solid as the ground under his feet. He knew when he asked the Creator for wine, the water fermented as soon as he asked. There's got to be a catch, right? I'm only human, flesh and blood. How can I possibly be a manifestation of the Divine in spite of my humanity? No catch; it is Spirit's nature to give us anything we ask for. *Anything?* Yes, even asking a dead man to rise. The only roadblock I ever face is my lack of belief. There has been at least one moment for each of us when we witnessed something and mumbled, "Unbelievable." We saw it; we heard it, but we couldn't fathom it was possible.

Well, believe it. Each of us is here to walk on water. When my ego screams, "Me, me, me!" my Higher Self says, "I am my brother's keeper." We are one and the same. When my humanity says I have been wronged, my divinity says, I choose to forgive. When my fear says the world is a scary place, my Creator says, "Allow me to remove the blinders from your eyes. Behold! The Kingdom is at hand." *Matthew 3:2* Divine Spirit within me, you transform the unbelievable into reality.

I Am Unbelievable . . .

I Am Valuable

"Act as though I am and I will be."
Science of Mind, p. 295

I remember the day my childhood hero told me I was worthless and would never amount to anything. Those words sliced through me like a knife. His part was speaking to me that way. My part was taking those words and draping them over my shoulders like a cloak of victimhood. *If I was going to be worthless, I would be the best bleepin' worthless guy this world has ever seen.* It was arrogant and egotistical of me. While my peers said come join us in this endeavor called life, I chose to sit in my corner and play the "worthless" game.

Sometimes a person gets sick and tired of being sick and tired. My pity party never benefitted God, myself or the rest of the world. How does one turn around years of self-centered behavior? For every person who loved me before I was capable of loving myself, "Thank you" does not suffice. It is ironic that in order to recognize my own value, I had to acknowledge the value in others first. My mentors and peers taught me that it is an honor to serve. As I serve, I am served. As I give, so I receive. Namaste; the divinity within me recognizes and honors the divinity within you. As Spirit gradually revealed to me the God qualities within others, I remembered who and what I am. Divine Spirit within me, thank you for the opportunity to be your face, hands and feet in the here and now. "It is not I, but the Father that doeth the works." *John 14:10*

I Am Valuable . . .

I Am Whole

"We are so one with the whole that what is true of it is also true of us."
Science of Mind, p. 195

In the movie, *Jerry Maguire*, Cruise says to Zellweger, "You complete me." Man, people ate that stuff up, and yes, I am guilty as charged. I never felt like a whole, complete person in and of myself. Over the years, I've tried every selfish, self-seeking endeavor you can imagine to feel complete. I sought fulfilment in a relationship. I thought if I could succeed at being a human doing, I would get the satisfaction and contentment I longed for. To no avail; nothing worked, and I continued to feel empty. I would love to say I had some fancy, spectacular transformation. The truth is, I lost everything; the relationship, the job, all my possessions. I remember the day I stood with nothing but four walls around me. In that moment, the Spirit within me said, "Right here, right now, you have exactly what you came into this world with and you'll leave this world with the exact same thing; me. In that moment of nothingness, I realized I had everything. I acknowledged my divinity within had always been with me. It is within me now and will always be with me. Spirit within, you are the source of my breath. You are the source of my life. Divine Spirit within me, you are my only constant. It is you that completes me.

I Am Whole . . .

I AM X

When Moses asked the Creator, "Who shall I say has sent me," the Creator simply said, I Am. How does one describe that which cannot be fully described? For centuries there have been countless names used to try and describe our Creator. There is no way human language and/or written word can completely define God. My purpose for writing this book has been to share my experience of the Great I Am up to this point in my process. It has also been an opportunity to reveal the Great I Am I have witnessed in others. I could write a million books and not have the God thing figured out 100 percent. Everyone loves a good mystery. We read mystery novels; we watch mystery shows on TV; we buy movie tickets to watch mysteries at the theatre. In spite of this, you and I get frustrated when we don't understand ourselves, each other, life. I have friends I've known most of my life, and I'm still getting to know that person. The joy of our friendship is a mystery that continues to unfold. Each of us never knows for sure what the other may say or do. Our maker loves a good mystery, as well. The Spirit within us waits with bated breath to see what we may create, express, manifest.

Embrace the mystery within yourself. Embrace the mystery within each other. Embrace the mystery in life. Divine Spirit within me, as this mystery continues to unfold, I am ready to start the next chapter.

I Am X . . .

I AM YOUTH

"And so we prepare not to die, but to live."
Science of Mind, p. 388

Many times I have heard someone say, "It sucks getting old." The gradual breakdown of the human body is extremely challenging. It is never appropriate to make light of this process. In 1993, the late Jim Valvano gave an amazing speech at the ESPY Awards show. Facing terminal cancer, his talk focused on life, not death. He encouraged all of us to fully embrace life through laughter, emotion and contemplation. The Spirit within him declared to the world, "Cancer cannot touch my mind, my heart, my soul." Whenever I'm having a tough day, I can listen to his talk, and my attitude turns 180 degrees. My mentors and peers have taught me I'm responsible for my quality of life. My attitude determines the level of quality. His Holiness, the Dalai Lama is no spring chicken. Yet, his smile, his laugh, the twinkle in his eye reflects the Divine youth within him. Divine youth is timeless. I have worked at assisted living facilities for senior citizens. I have witnessed Spirit's wit, wisdom and humor within these people who are in the later stages of life. They have not shown me how to die; they have shown me how to live. Approach each day like you are squeezing water from a sponge; don't waste a single drop. Laugh, cry, kick and cuss your way through life like no one will ever forget. Have people tell stories about you long after you've left this earth.

Youthful Spirit within, may your childlike zest for life be evident in my thoughts, my words, my deeds.

I Am Youth . . .

I Am Zeus

"I have said ye are Gods." (Psalms 82:6),

Science of Mind, p. 364

I have enjoyed reading Greek Mythology since I was a child. Aphrodite, the Goddess of Love and Beauty, Athena, the Goddess of Wisdom and Courage—these characters are a part of our culture to this day. Many movies have been made about the super strong, Hercules. "Hotter than Hades," and "my Achilles heel" are common terms. When I was younger, I would long to be like these extraordinary characters. I would chalk up my daydreaming to wishful thinking. *I'm just a lowly human,* I kept telling myself. The greatest sin I have ever committed is self-hatred. Out of this stems all my transgressions against myself and others. I needed a brand new belief system. Each of us is a Spiritual being having a human experience. *Pierre Teilhard de Chardin* Every man, woman and child possesses these Zeus-like qualities. I realize I'm surrounded by Gods. No greater example than the person who faces cancer with dignity and grace. Because this person chooses victory instead of playing the victim, all those God-like qualities are brought to the forefront. There is no Achilles heel in this person's walk. Each of us was sent here to walk among the Gods. What does this look like for you?

When my Creator pushes my pen across this paper, a fire within me burns at a level Hades can only dream of. Allow the voice of Zeus within you; announce to the world, Spirit is, I am and we are!

I Am Zeus . . .

Printed in the United States
by Baker & Taylor Publisher Services